Thank you to my husband! We are so glad we can always count on you! Thank you for sharing miles of adventures with us!

Thank you to St. Charles Vet Clinic for helping keep the energetic puppies happy and healthy.

Thank you to my amazing pack of pups! Who inspire me with their crazy antics, boundless energy and never ending curiosity.

Copyright © 2025 Elizabeth Lloyd
ISBN: 979-8-9885067-4-4
Library of Congress Control Number: 2025907287
Publisher's Cataloging-in-Publication Data

Names: Lloyd, Elizabeth Ann, author.
Title: Huskies explore numbers and counting / by Elizabeth Lloyd
Description: Eyota, MN: Elizabeth Lloyd, 2025. | Summary: Huskies explore and count numbers 1-20.
Identifiers: LCCN: 2025907287 | ISBN: 979-8-9885067-4-4
Subjects: LCSH Counting--Juvenile literature. | Numeration--Juvenile literature. | Dogs--Juvenile literature. | BISAC JUVENILE NONFICTION / Concepts / Counting & Numbers | JUVENILE NONFICTION Animals / Dogs
Classification: LCC QA41 .L56 Hu 2025 | DDC 510.1/48--dc23

Huskies Explore Numbers and Counting

Elizabeth Lloyd

The Huskies love to explore. They are curious about numbers. A perfect adventure for the energetic Huskies.

Counting is fun! Start with one. Add another and you get two. This is easy for you!

We can count forever just by adding one more, but that would be a lot to explore.

The Huskies are going to count numbers one to twenty. That should be plenty.

Counting is fun, there is no doubt, but the Huskies might need a little help!

We are so glad you are on this adventure with us!

One 1

2 Two

Three

Four

Five 5

six 6

Eight

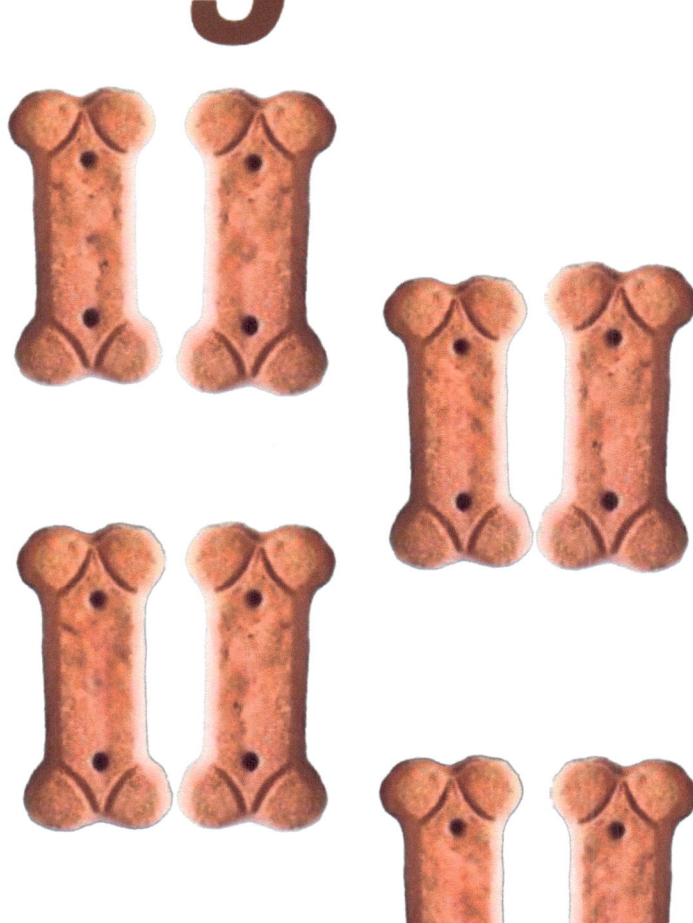

10 Ten

Ten 10

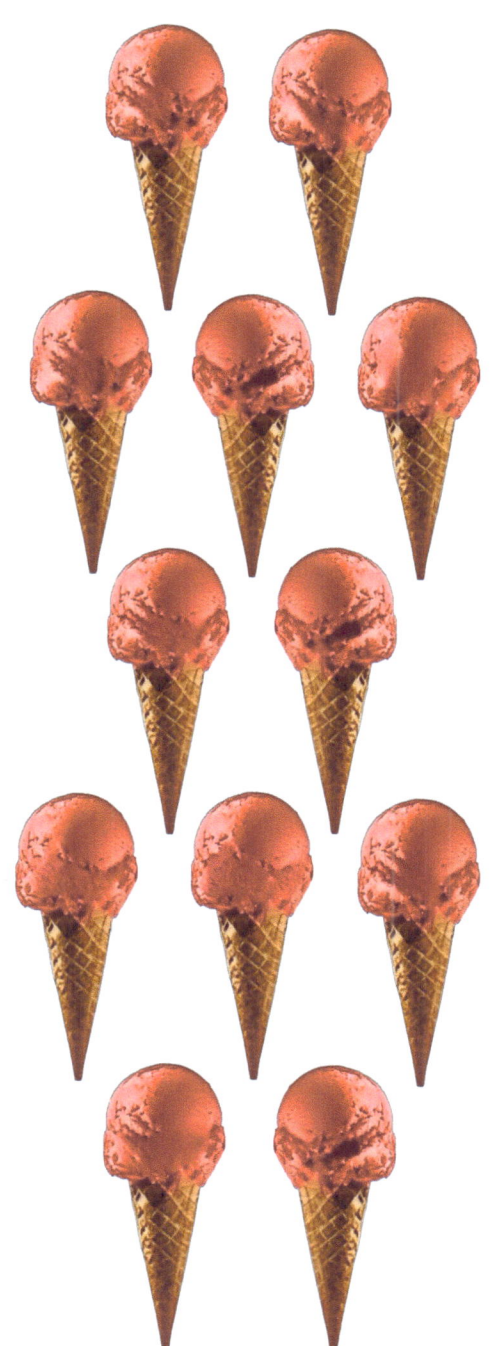

Twelve
12

13 Thirteen

Thirteen
13

14 Fourteen

Fourteen 14

15 Fifteen

Fifteen 15

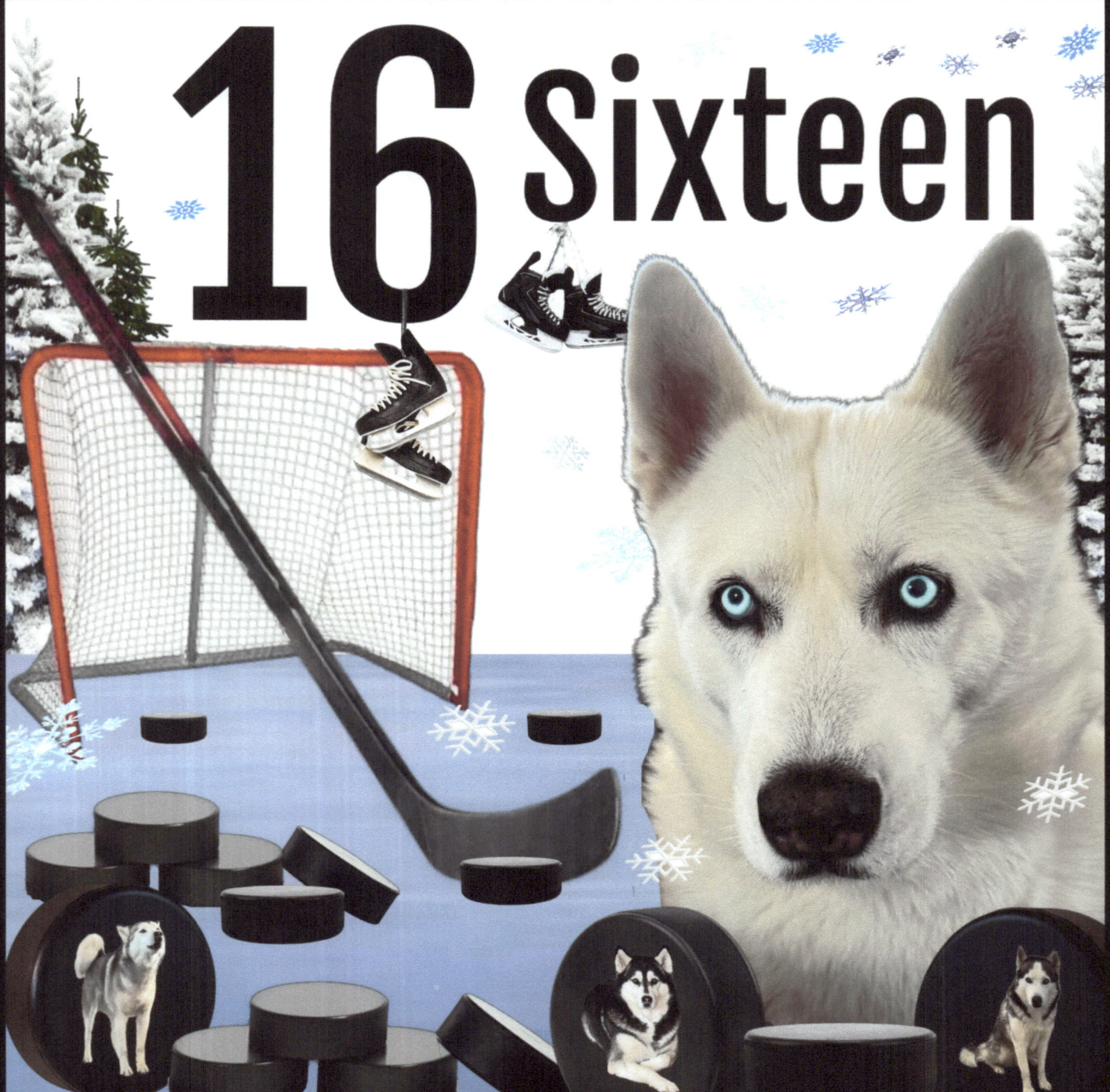

Sixteen 16

Seventeen 17

18 Eighteen

Eighteen 18

Nineteen 19

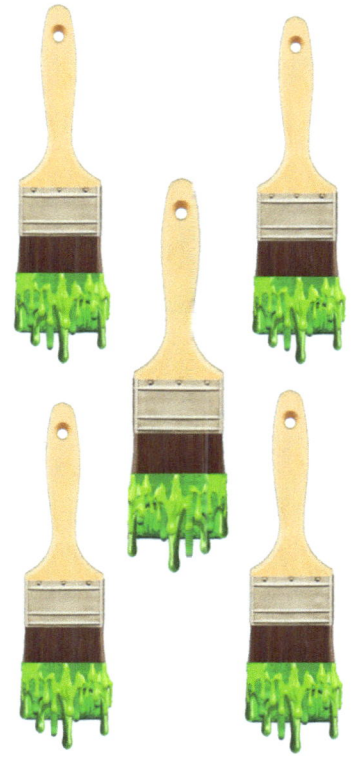

Twenty 20

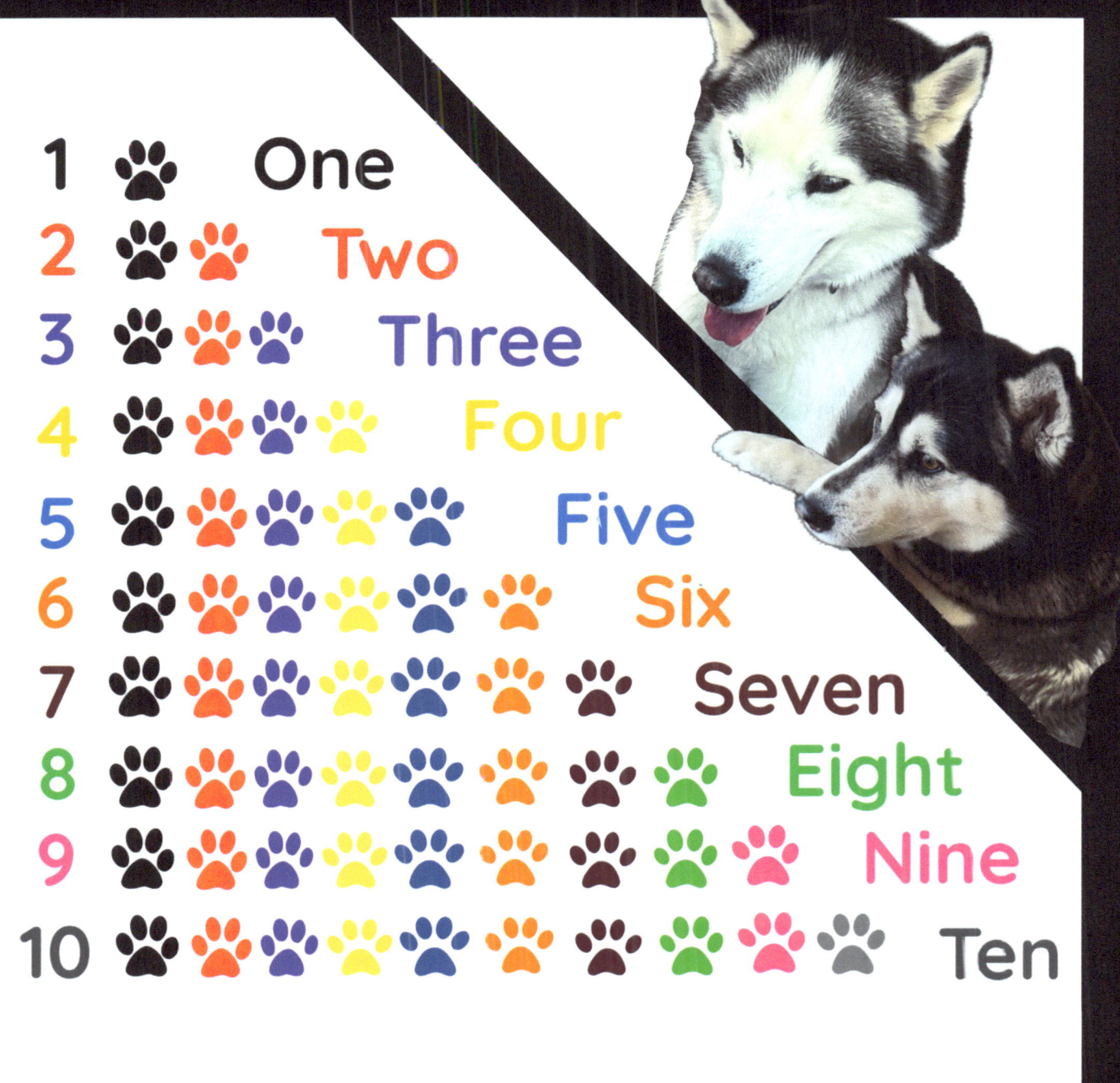

Thank you for exploring numbers and counting with us!

See you on our next adventure!